BIBLE
VERSE
COLORING
BOOK

THIS BOOK
BELONGS
TO

How to use this book

This is a Bible Verse Coloring Book
for kids to learn how to paint
and identify colors, using
inspirational and key scripture
verses from the Bible
that will inspire
them and deepen their faith
to the Lord.

Users can test the colors on
the next page, and paint each
element using their preferred
color. So grab your colored
pencils and start spending
some time with the Lord.

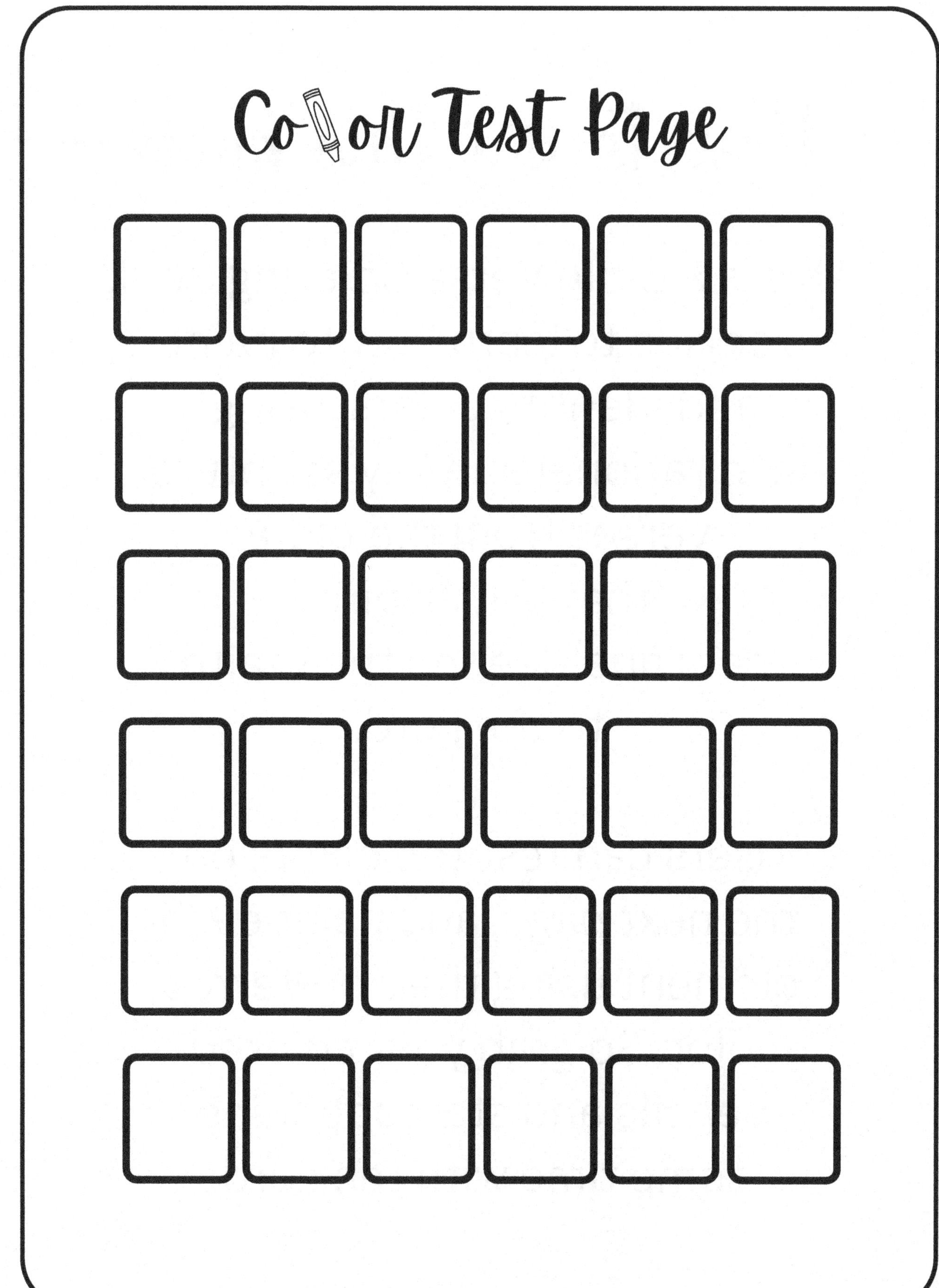
Color Test Page

Faith without works is Dead
James 2:26

Children are an heritage of the Lord
PSALM 127:3

In everything give thanks
1 Thessalonians 5:18

The Lord
bless thee
and keep
thee.
Numbers 6:24

Let everything that has breath praise the Lord. Psalm 150:6

I am
with you
always
Matthew 28:20

The heavens declare the glory of God
Psalm 19:1

TRUST IN
THE LORD
WITH ALL
THINE
HEART
Proverbs 3:5

Jesus wept.
John 11:35

We ought to obey God rather than Men
Acts 5:29

Every good gift
and every
perfect gift
is from above.
James 1:17

We love him, because he first loved us.

1 John 4:19

PRAY
WITHOUT
CEASING
1 THESSALONIANS
5:17

FOR THE
LORD GIVETH
WISDOM
PROVERBS 2:6

HE IS NOT HERE

HE IS RISEN

Matthew 28:6

BUT THE WAY
OF THE
UNGODLY
SHALL
PERISH.
Psalm 1:6

Fear not:
for I am
with thee
Isaiah 43:5

I will praise thee;
for I am fearfully
and wonderfully
made.
Psalm 139:14

WHATSOEVER
YE DO,
DO ALL
TO THE
GLORY
OF GOD.
1 CORINTHIANS 10:31

No man
can serve
two
masters
Matthew 6:24

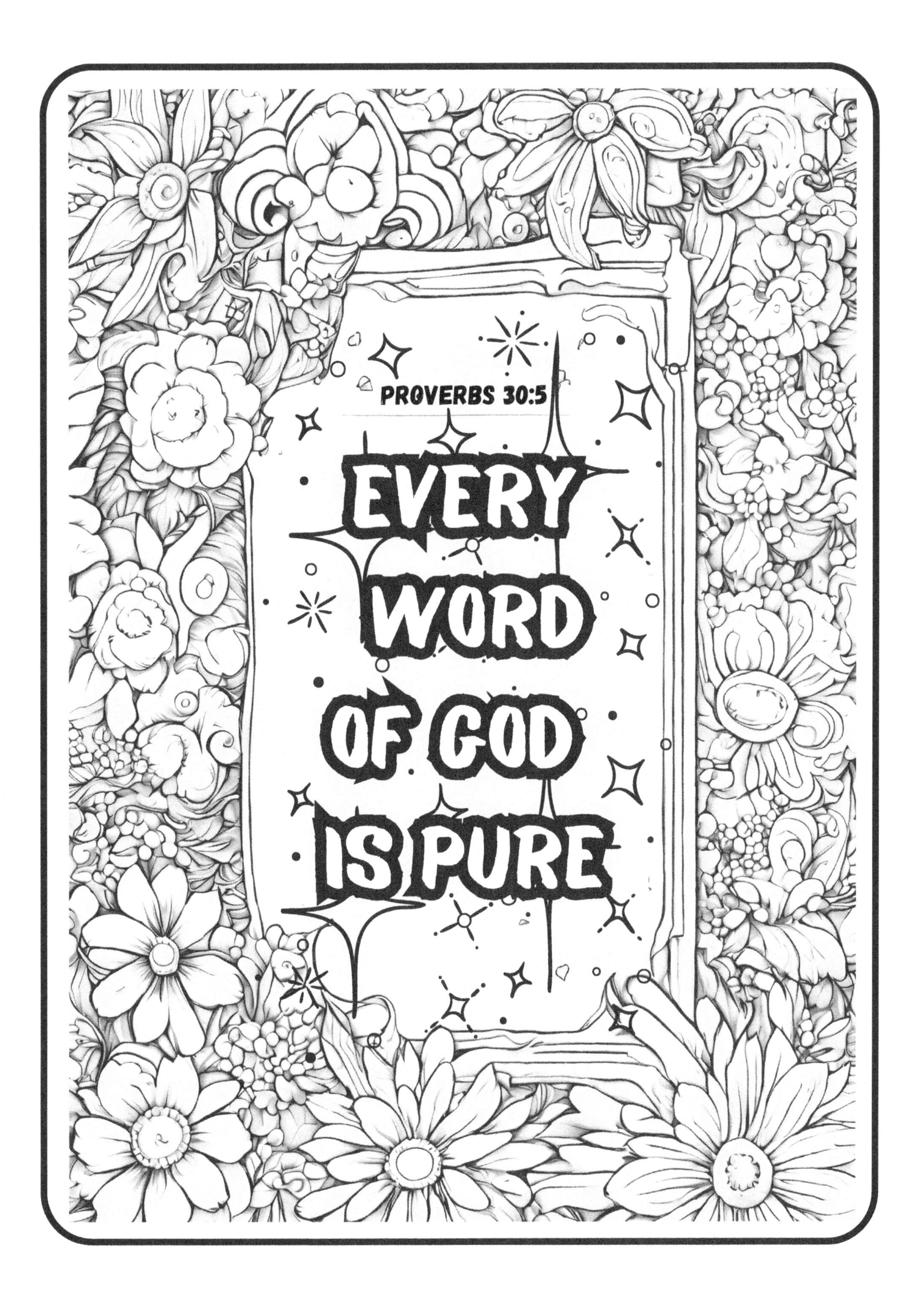
PROVERBS 30:5
EVERY
WORD
OF GOD
IS PURE

Children, obey
your parents in
the Lord:
for this is
right
EPHESIANS 6:1

Psalm 118:24
THIS IS
THE DAY
WHICH
THE
LORD
HATH
MADE

Thy word
HOLY
BIBLE
is a lamp
unto my
feet, and
a light
unto
Psalm 119:105
my path

What time I am
afraid, I will
trust in thee.
Psalm 56:3

A FAITHFUL WITNESS WILL NOT LIE

PROVERBS 14:5

Set your
affections on
things above
Colossians 3:2

YE ARE THE
LIGHT OF
THE
WORLD
MATTHEW
5:14

Jesus Christ
the same
yesterday, and
today, and
for ever.
Hebrews 13:8

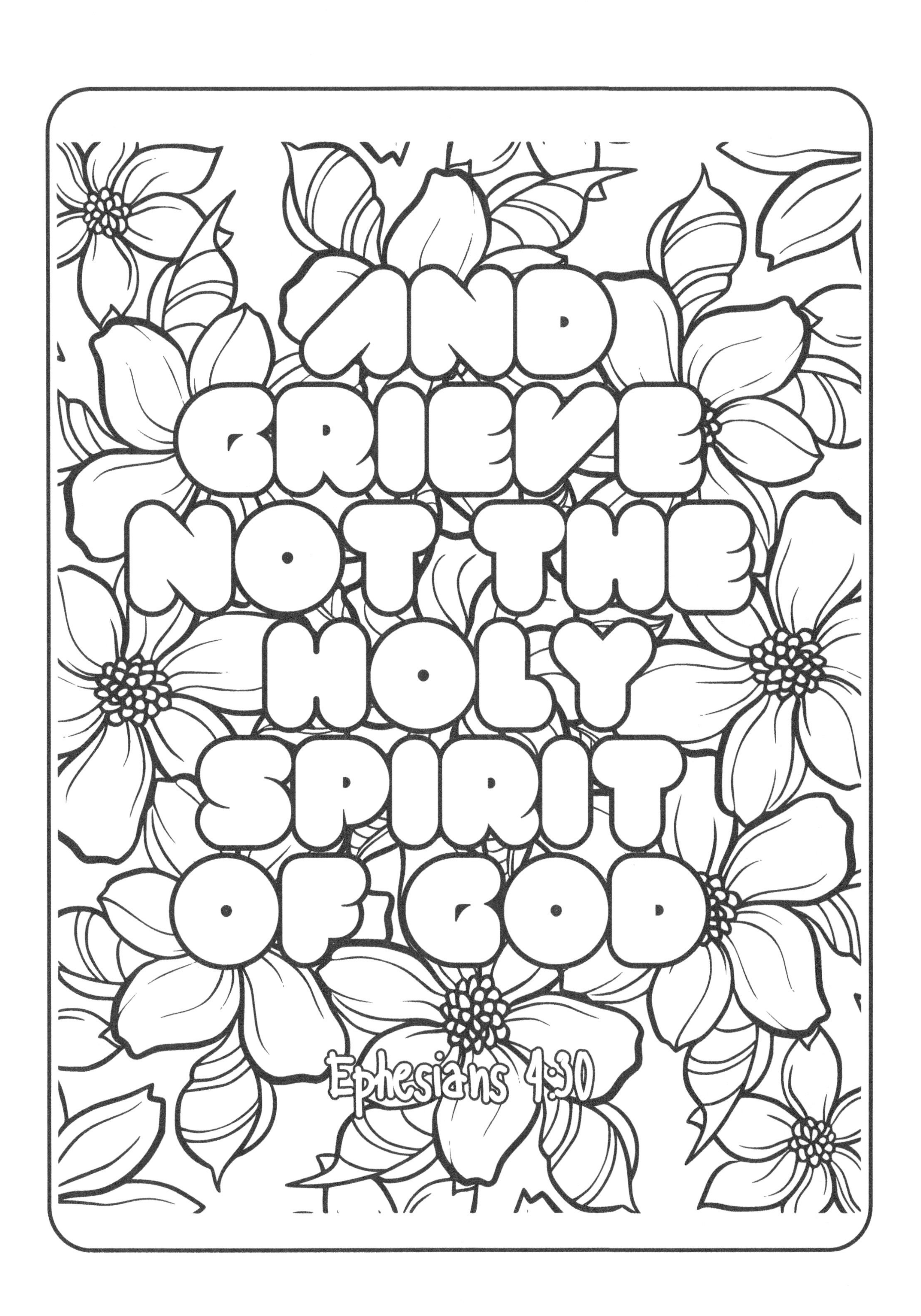
AND
GRIEVE
NOT THE
HOLY
SPIRIT
OF GOD
Ephesians 4:30

For all have sinned and
come short of the glory
of God.
Romans 3:23

In the beginning
God created
the heaven
and the
earth.
Genesis 1:1

BE STILL AND KNOW THAT I AM GOD

Psalm 46:10

Romans 12:18

STUDY TO

SHEW THYSELF

APPROVED

UNTO GOD

2 Timothy 2:15

REJOICETH IN THE

TRUTH

1 CORINTHIANS 13:6

THIS IS THE confidence
WE HAVE IN APPROACHING
God: THAT IF WE ASK
ANYTHING ACCORDING
TO HIS will,
HE heareth
US.

1 JOHN 5:14

GOD IS OUR REFUGE AND STRENGTH, A VERY PRESENT HELP IN TROUBLE

PSALM 46:1

Surely goodness
and mercy
shall follow
me all the
days of my
life.
PSALM 23:6

And I will dwell
in the house
of the LORD
for ever
PSALM 23:6

Made in United States
Orlando, FL
20 September 2024

51758921R00050